Getting To Know...

Nature's Children

GROUSE

John B. Théberge
and
Mary T. Théberge

PUBLISHER   Joseph R. DeVarennes

PUBLICATION DIRECTOR   Kenneth H. Pearson

MANAGING EDITOR   Valerie Wyatt

SERIES ADVISOR   Merebeth Switzer

SERIES CONSULTANT   Michael Singleton

CONSULTANTS   Ross James
Kay McKeever
Dr. Audrey N. Tomera

ADVISORS   Roger Aubin
Robert Furlonger
Gaston Lavoie

EDITORIAL SUPERVISOR   Jocelyn Smyth

PRODUCTION MANAGER   Ernest Homewood

PRODUCTION ASSISTANTS   Penelope Moir
Brock Piper

EDITORS   Katherine Farris   Anne Minguet-Patocka
Sandra Gulland   Sarah Reid
Cristel Kleitsch   Cathy Ripley
Elizabeth MacLeod   Eleanor Tourtel
Pamela Martin   Karin Velcheff

PHOTO EDITORS   Bill Ivy
Don Markle

DESIGN   Annette Tatchell

CARTOGRAPHER   Jane Davie

PUBLICATION ADMINISTRATION   Kathy Kishimoto
Monique Lemonnier

ARTISTS   Marianne Collins   Greg Ruhl
Pat Ivy   Mary Theberge

This series is approved and recommended by the Federation of Ontario Naturalists.

Canadian Cataloguing in Publication Data

Theberge, John B., 1940-
  Grouse

(Getting to know—nature's children)
Includes index.
ISBN 0-7172-1931-3

1. Grouse—Juvenile literature.
I. Theberge, Mary T. II. Title. III. Series.

QL696.G285T48 1985   j598'.616   C85-098715-6

Have you ever wondered . . .

Usually taking a walk in the forest in spring is a quiet thing to do. But not if there are grouse nearby! Hoots or booming or thudding sounds, made by male grouse trying to attract females, will rock the quiet.

Being noisy is not the only unusual characteristic of grouse. Did you know that some grouse also:

- sleep in snowbanks
- would rather walk than fly
- eat about 30 meals a day when they are young
- leave the nest an hour after hatching.

What unusual birds grouse are! Let's find out more about them.

The origin of the word grouse *is uncertain but many people think it comes from an old French word meaning "spotted bird." (Ruffed Grouse)*

A Ping Pong Ball With Legs

Imagine a ball, small enough to hold in your cupped hands. A ping pong ball will do. Think of it covered in soft down, with two tiny, scratchy feet, a little knob of a head and wriggling all over. There you have it—a grouse chick! Small black eyes peek out from its downy head, a stubby beak points into the air, but with no wing feathers or tail it looks unfinished, like a human baby born bald and without eyebrows.

Put the little chick on the ground and away it goes, a ball of fluff zooming off to find its mother.

The mother grouse is very near and calling loudly. While you were holding the chick, she flopped across the ground as if her wing was broken. She was trying to attract your attention and trick you into chasing after her so that you would leave her chicks alone. Grouse learned to do this a long time ago to give their chicks a chance to escape.

What Is a Grouse?

Grouse are one of the three families of chicken-like birds found in North America. The other two are the pheasant family (which includes the domestic chicken) and the turkey family.

There are nine kinds of grouse in North America. They have certain things in common which distinguish them from other chicken-like birds. They all have feathers on their face that completely hide their nostrils, which are located at the base of their beak. They also have completely or partly feathered legs. The rest of their wild chicken relatives wear shorts instead of pants—their legs are bare.

Grouse tails.

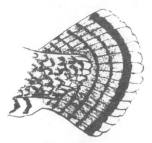

Ruffed Grouse.

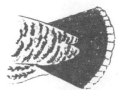

Spruce Grouse.

Sharp-tailed Grouse.

The Ruffed Grouse is named for the black ruff, or collar, around its neck.

A Grouse by Any Other Name

Many people call the grouse a partridge, but they are wrong. However, some kinds of grouse do go by other names, so it is no wonder that people are sometimes confused. Some kinds of grouse are called Prairie Chickens, while others are called ptarmigans (pronounced **tar**-mi-gans).

Ptarmigans are different from other grouse. They have feathers all the way down to the tips of their toes (Willow Ptarmigan)

Grouse Everywhere

There are grouse in all parts of North America and, in fact, all over the world. Some live on prairies, others prefer forests, and others are found on the treeless arctic tundra. There is a type of grouse for every habitat.

If you took a walk in the woods, the grouse you saw would probably be a Ruffed Grouse. It is the most common grouse, and it is found in the most places. You can even find Ruffed Grouse in woodlots or ravines near large cities.

The Spruce Grouse and the Blue Grouse also live in forests. As you might guess, the Prairie Chicken is found on the prairies or in deserts. You will also find the Sharp-tailed and Sage Grouse living there.

Up north on the arctic tundra live the ptarmigans—the White-tailed, Rock and Willow Ptarmigan. What a big family the grouse family is!

Sage Grouse can be identified by their very distinctive tail.

Why Fly?

Grouse fly very little. They prefer to stay on the ground. This is where they find their food. Some grouse may climb trees. The Ruffed Grouse is an especially good climber. It can even climb up thin bendy stems.

All grouse can fly, but they are often awkward at taking off. To get airborne, a grouse must flap furiously. Compared to most other birds, it has a slow and noisy take-off.

Blue Grouse, like all grouse, would much rather walk than fly.

Grouse Disappearing Act

Many animals would love a grouse dinner.

Hawks and owls eat grouse. These predators like to perch on the horizontal branches of pine, hemlock and other trees that provide them with good footing. So survival rule one for grouse is: stay away from these trees. Rule two is to stay in dense tangles of brush and small trees into which hawks and owls have trouble swooping.

Foxes, martens and lynx eat grouse too, and they move like lightning. How does a grouse avoid being eaten by these land-based predators?

It has special protective coloring to help it blend in with its surroundings. This is called camouflage. Depending on where they live, grouse may be dark brown to gray to red, often with lighter speckles. This makes them difficult to see in most surroundings.

To make their disappearing act even more effective, grouse may freeze like statues if they sense danger. Motionless and camouflaged, they are well hidden from enemies.

Opposite page:

You need sharp eyes to spot the Rock Ptarmigan hiding here. It looks so much like a rock!

Different Colors

How can a grouse known as the Blue Grouse blend into its surroundings? Do not be fooled by its name. The Blue Grouse is not actually blue. Its feathers are a dusky bluish gray, and this color blends in well with its mountain home.

Another grouse, the ptarmigan, changes color twice a year. For the winter, when the tundra will be covered with snow, it grows white feathers. In spring, it grows a new coat of brown and white speckled feathers. These make it hard to see against the brown of the summer tundra.

In spring and fall, when the ptarmigan's new feathers are growing in, it is half brown and half white. You might think that this would make it easy to spot, but in fact its two-tone coat is good protection. It blends in perfectly with the brown and white snow-patched tundra!

Blue Grouse.

Early Warning System

Since the grouse relies on camouflage and keeping still to avoid predators, it needs an early warning system to tell it when danger is nearby. The grouse's sense of smell is not very good, but it does have excellent eyesight. It can see even a slight movement that you would probably miss. If it has time, the grouse will take off and fly away. If not, it will freeze and hope the predator overlooks it.

A grouse's sharp eyes don't miss much. (Ruffed Grouse)

Salad Anyone?

Put some young shoots of grass in a bowl.
Add some buds of shrubs, some seeds, berries
and a few twigs, and a grouse would gladly
come to dinner. The food value of all these
things is high. But if you do not think such a
salad would be very tasty, you could toss in
some beetles, flies, snails, spiders and ants.
Chicks especially, when very young, like
animal food, but as they grow older, they eat
more plants.

The menu for grouse is much shorter in
winter than it is in summer. With some
species, the daily special never changes. For
Ruffed Grouse it is the buds of aspen trees.
Energy is packed into these buds to help form
new leaves in spring. Ruffed Grouse get more
energy for each beakful by eating buds than they
could get from anything else they can find.

For Spruce Grouse, the winter diet is almost
always the same—spruce needles. Only now
and then will they try something else, such as
needles of balsam fir or jack pine.

Opposite page:

*Spruce Grouse are
so absurdly tame
that they have
earned the
nickname "fool
hen."*

Do Grouse Have Teeth?

No member of the grouse family has teeth, yet they still manage to chew their food. How do they do it? And why don't the sharp needles and twigs that they eat scratch their stomachs? The answer is that, like all birds, grouse have a special stomach, or gizzard, with a horny lining that grinds up their food. And like many birds, grouse pick up small pebbles and swallow them. The pebbles stay in their gizzard to help break up needles and other hard food.

There is nothing more refreshing to a grouse than a good dust bath. (Spruce Grouse)

A Bed of Snow

Grouse do not fly south in winter as many birds do. Nor do they have special dens to curl up in. They live outside all winter long. Put yourself in the grouse's place and imagine what winter in the north must be like. During the daytime, you might be warmed by the sun. And you would be moving around to find food and that would warm you up a little. But what about at night? Winter nights can be long and cold, especially if there is no warm bed to snuggle into.

But grouse do have a warm bed. On really cold nights, when the temperature drops far below freezing, they sleep in the snow to keep from freezing too. Although a snow bed is not as warm as you might like, it is often a lot warmer than the outside air.

A Ruffed Grouse getting into its snow bed is an amazing sight. At dusk, it simply dives from its tree perch head first into a nearby snowbank. There it burrows in for the night. In the morning it bobs up after a good night's rest.

Opposite page:

Willow Ptarmigan in winter plumage.

Snowshoe Champs

Deep snow could be a problem for a bird that spends so much of its time on the ground. However, grouse do not get bogged down when walking on snow because their feet can act like built-in snowshoes.

A grouse's long toes have tough ridges along them that spread out over the snow, spreading the bird's weight over a wide area and helping to keep it on top of the snow. Ptarmigans go even further. They have feathers on their toes—their own special brand of snowshoes.

Snowshoe-like foot of Ruffed Grouse.

Walking on the snow is no problem for a Ruffed Grouse.

Flashy Display

Each spring, many male grouse try to claim a piece of territory as their own. They stake out this territory by putting on a show. This is called displaying. Grouse also display to attract females to their territory. These displays begin in the early spring and last for more than a month during the mating season.

Each kind of grouse has its own special way of displaying. But whatever the display, there is one thing you can be certain of: it is noisy!

Male Ruffed Grouse displaying.

Wild Drummer

Ruffed Grouse drum. Thud, thud, thud . . . slowly at first, then faster and faster until it dies away in a muffled roll. To make this thudding sound, the male stands up on a log and pumps the air with his wings. At the end of a series of drums, his wings are going so fast they they are a blur. Then he stops, fans out his tail, raises his dark neck feathers and stands looking handsome for about half a minute. Two or three minutes later, he is drumming again.

The Ruffed Grouse's show begins early in the morning. Each male has his own special log where he displays. As the day warms up, he will stop and go looking for food. But in the evening, he may be back displaying until dark.

A male Ruffed Grouse will sometimes use the same "drumming" log year after year.

Noisy Boomers and Hooters

Instead of drumming, Prairie Chickens boom. On a hill-top dancing ground, the males strut back and forth in front of each other, with neck feathers raised around two orange-colored air pouches on their chest. They inflate these pouches, then send the air rushing out in a series of loud booms that carry across the open grasslands.

The Prairie Chicken display is held at the same place every morning. As many as 20 males join in to try to impress the females. Now and then the dancers pounce at each other between displays, fighting for the chance to display in the center of the group.

Other kinds of grouse hoot, making the mountain valleys echo with their calls. Or they make wild flights high over the tundra, cackling loudly, then diving to the ground.

No matter how a grouse displays, the message is clear. To other males the display says "Stay out of my territory." To females it says "Here I am." Females watch or listen and pick the male they think is best.

Opposite page:

What a show off!
(Blue Grouse)

A Lot of Eggs

After mating, most female grouse build nests
in hollows on the ground. Sheltered places at
the base of a tree or large rock or by a log or
brushpile are often chosen. Some nests are
built of sticks and leaves, often lined with pine
needles or grasses and some downy feathers
from the mother's breast. Others are just bits
of dirt and stones scraped into a rough circle.

The mother grouse lays one egg a day. They
are light beige, sometimes spotted with brown.
The total number a mother lays depends on
her health. If she ate well during the late
winter, she may lay as many as 14 eggs. This
sounds like a lot, but she may lose some to
bad weather or to predators such as weasels or
ravens. If she loses the entire clutch of eggs,
she may lay another clutch.

*The Ruffed Grouse is not a very good
nest builder. Its nest is often little
more than a slight depression in the
forest floor.*

Happy Hatchday

The mother grouse begins to incubate, or sit on, her eggs only after the last one is laid. That way all the chicks hatch at the same time, so she can look after them better and give them all an equal chance for survival. Each day she turns the eggs with her beak so that all parts of the eggs are warmed.

About 23 days after incubation begins, the chicks peck a ring around the large end of their egg with their "egg tooth," a bump on their beak used for this purpose. They begin to call to their mother even before they have broken completely away from their shells. Then out they crawl.

The days of rest for the mother grouse are over! Suddenly she has a lot of hungry, squirmy, cheepy chicks to keep warm and watch over.

Within twelve hours all the rest of this mother grouse's babies will have hatched. (Ruffed Grouse)

Bright Babies

Grouse chicks are not like most baby birds. They leave the nest within an hour of hatching and never return. They can already run as fast as their mother, and except for needing some extra warmth now and then, they are quite capable of taking care of themselves.

Right from the start, the grouse chicks recognize what is good to eat. They know that a particular high, thin call from their mother means danger is near, and they should freeze, and they know that another call means for them to come running. They recognize danger too—anything moving that is larger than themselves.

How do they know all this without being taught? By instinct. This means they are born with the information they need for their survival already stored in the brains.

The hour-old grouse chicks cannot fly, however. For that, they will have to wait three or four weeks, until their wing and tail feathers have grown.

Opposite page:

Young Sharp-tailed Grouse.

Warmth or Food?

Although they can look after themselves in many ways, grouse chicks do have a problem for the first few days of their life. They get cold and must huddle close to their mother for warmth. But just when they start to feel nice and comfortable, hunger strikes. Off they go, pecking at seeds and buds, spiders, flies, almost anything. About one out of every three beakfuls of food is insects.

But then—brrr! They are cold again. So they go running back to their mother to warm up.

Soon they will be hungry again. And so it goes, all day long. Grouse chicks must fill their stomachs about 30 times a day. They will double in weight during their first five or six days, so they need lots of food.

Climbing over these rocks is quite a feat for this little ptarmigan chick.

Family Days

Grouse chicks are good babies. They come when their mother calls them. They follow her closely and never quarrel with each other.

In the mornings, grouse families wander along together, eating continuously. They spend afternoons resting in the shelter of trees or shrubs. In the evening they are active once more, but as twilight ends they again take shelter.

In most cases, the father does not stay with his family. He lives alone on or near his territory. Male Willow Ptarmigans, however, stay with their brood and help protect the chicks by flying at and attacking any enemy.

The male Willow Ptarmigan is a faithful father.

On Their Own

By autumn the chicks are almost fully grown. Their baby down has been shed and feathers have grown in. These new feathers help trap body-warmed air close to their skin and keep them warm.

This is the time when most grouse families break up. Only ptarmigan on the tundra stay in flocks. Other young grouse wander away from their parents and each other, traveling five to ten kilometres (3-6 miles) to find a good place to begin their own lives. They spend the long, cold winter alone.

At last spring comes again. The snow melts and the days warm. Some of the young grouse now find their own territories, display and mate. Others wait until they are two years old.

Everywhere grouse are displaying—out on the prairies, up on the tundra or down in the corner woodlot. And as spring turns to summer, in every wild area across the land, grouse chicks will hatch. Soon they too will join the other drummers, hooters and boomers of the grouse family.

Special Words

Camouflage Marking or coloring that helps an animal blend in with its surroundings.

Clutch A group of eggs.

Display The special pattern of behavior a bird uses to attract a mate or claim a territory.

Egg tooth A tooth-like point on the end of a chick's bill that it uses to help it break out of its egg.

Gizzard The part of a bird's stomach where food is ground up, often with the help of small stones.

Habitat The area or type of area in which an animal or plant naturally lives.

Incubate To sit on the eggs and keep them warm so that the chicks inside can grow.

Mate To come together to produce young.

Nostrils Openings through which air is taken into the body.

Predator An animal that hunts other animals for food.

Territory Area of land that an animal or group of animals lives in and often defends against other animals of the same kind.

Tundra Flat land in the Arctic where no trees grow.

INDEX

Cover Photo: Wayne Lankinen (Valan Photos)

Photo Credits: Bill Ivy, page 4; George Peck, pages 7, 20, 39; Arthur Savage, page 8; Stephen J. Krasemann (Valan Photos), page 11; Wilf Schurig (Valan Photos), page 12; Dennis Schmidt (Valan Photos), page 15; John Théberge, pages 16, 32; Thomas Kitchin (Valan Photos), pages 19, 24; Hälle Flygare (Valan Photos), page 23; Wayne Lankinen (Valan Photos), pages 27, 28; Tom W. Parkin (Valan Photos), page 35; Robert C. Simpson (Valan Photos), page 36; W. Schiels (Valan Photos), page 40; B. Lyon (Valan Photos), page 43; James Richards, page 44.

Getting To Know...

Nature's Children

MUSKOX

Merebeth Switzer

PUBLISHER	Joseph R. DeVarennes
PUBLICATION DIRECTOR	Kenneth H. Pearson
MANAGING EDITOR	Valerie Wyatt
SERIES ADVISOR	Merebeth Switzer
SERIES CONSULTANT	Michael Singleton
CONSULTANTS	Ross James
	Kay McKeever
	Dr. Audrey N. Tomera
ADVISORS	Roger Aubin
	Robert Furlonger
	Gaston Lavoie
EDITORIAL SUPERVISOR	Jocelyn Smyth
PRODUCTION MANAGER	Ernest Homewood
PRODUCTION ASSISTANTS	Penelope Moir
	Brock Piper

EDITORS

Katherine Farris	Anne Minguet-Patocka
Sandra Gulland	Sarah Reid
Cristel Kleitsch	Cathy Ripley
Elizabeth MacLeod	Eleanor Tourtel
Pamela Martin	Karin Velcheff

PHOTO EDITORS	Bill Ivy
	Don Markle
DESIGN	Annette Tatchell
CARTOGRAPHER	Jane Davie
PUBLICATION ADMINISTRATION	Kathy Kishimoto
	Monique Lemonnier

ARTISTS

Marianne Collins	Greg Ruhl
Pat Ivy	Mary Theberge

This series is approved and recommended by the Federation of Ontario Naturalists.

Canadian Cataloguing in Publication Data

Switzer, Merebeth.
  Muskox

(Getting to know—nature's children)
Includes index.
ISBN 0-7172-1932-1

1. Musk ox—Juvenile literature.
I. Title. II. Series.

QL737.U53S97 1985   j599.73'58   C85-098724-5

Have you ever wondered . . .

Imagine visiting the Arctic in winter. Cold winds howl across the frozen tundra. Snow swirls all around. There is no sign of life. Or is there? Off in the distance are some huddled brown forms. What can they be?

They are muskoxen, gathered together to stay warm.

You have to be a pretty amazing animal to survive in a land where winter comes in September and stays until June. How can muskoxen stand the cold? Where do they find food in winter when snow blankets the ground?

Fortunately muskoxen are well-equipped for life in this frozen land.

Not an Ox at All

Do not be fooled by the muskox's name. It is not an ox at all. And it is not related to the bison either, though it looks rather like one. Instead, the muskox's closest relatives are goats.

Like goats, muskoxen are cud chewers. This means that they swallow their food whole, store it in a special part of their stomach and then bring it back to their mouth and chew it later. Muskoxen also have short goat-like tails, and they can climb like goats.

It is no mystery where the *musk* in the muskox's name came from. The male gives off a strong musky odor once a year when it is ready to mate.

But the muskox has another name that was given to it by the people who know it best. The Inuit call it Omingmak, meaning "the bearded one." One look at a muskox in its long, shaggy coat and you will see that this is a very good name.

The bearded one.

Living at the Ends of the Earth

Muskoxen once roamed all over the lands that surround the Arctic Ocean. They lived in Eurasia, Greenland, Alaska, mainland Canada and some of the Arctic Islands. But in the 1800s they were hunted for their meat and fur until they were nearly all gone.

Today muskoxen are protected. There are nearly 10 000 of them in northern Canada. They also occur naturally in Greenland and some have been taken to live in Iceland, the Soviet Union and Alaska.

Where muskoxen live in North America.

Even in summer, you would probably find Ellesmere Island beautiful but forbidding. To these muskoxen, it is home.

How Big?

In photographs, muskoxen often look enormous. But if you could visit them on the tundra, you would find that they are smaller than you might expect.

The shoulder hump of even a large adult male or bull would reach only to about your dad's chin. The muskox has a stocky body with short legs. The males can weigh from 200 to 400 kilograms (500 to 900 pounds). The females, or cows, weigh a little less than the bulls.

A bull's-eye view.

That Fantastic Fur Coat

Are you surprised to find that the muskox is not as big as you thought? Many people are fooled because the muskox's long, thick fur coat makes it look very big and bulky. Muskoxen probably have the longest hair of all wild animals, and they need it to keep them warm. Their coat also protects them from insects.

The hair is dark brown or almost black over most of the body, with a creamy to yellowish brown saddle-shaped marking on the back. The cows and young muskoxen have lighter hair on their foreheads.

The coat is curly at the shoulders, but hangs long and straight everywhere else. A muskox has especially thick, long hair at the front of its body. On windy winter days, it faces into the wind, so that this hair gets pressed tightly against its body, which helps keep in the heat.

Opposite page:

A super-thick coat has its uses even in summer. It protects the muskox from mosquitoes and flies.

Two Coats in One

What would you do if you had to face the freezing arctic winter without any shelter? First, you would make sure you had super-thick wool long-johns to put on under your outer clothing. Well, the muskox is admirably equipped in that department. Its fur coat is actually two coats in one.

The outer coat of long sleek guard hairs keeps out wind and blowing snow. Under this, grows a thick inner coat of soft fur. This warm, fine fleece completely covers the animal except for its lips and nostrils. Air warmed by the muskox's body gets trapped in this thick fleece.

And how would you keep your ears warm if you had to spend all winter out in the cold? Wear a hat? A muskox does not need a hat. Its ears are short and furry and fit closely to its body. They are almost impossible to see under its shaggy fur coat. The muskox's stubby tail is well hidden by warm fur too. Having small, furred ears and tail means the muskox loses less body heat through them.

Messy Shedder

In April or May the muskox starts to shed its fine inner coat. Gradually thick tufts of it work their way up through the heavy guard hairs.

If you saw a muskox at this time of year you might think it was sick. The fur hangs off the animal in big grayish brown clumps and makes the muskox look tattered and moth-eaten. Long pieces of fur blow in the wind. Some fur clumps stick to the rocks and bushes on which the muskoxen have rubbed themselves. But by mid-July the shedding is over, and the muskoxen have a new dark undercoat.

What happens to all the fur the muskoxen shed? Arctic birds use it to line their nests!

Changing clothes.

Keen Senses

Although the muskox's ears are almost buried in fur, it has a very keen sense of hearing.

You might also think that all that hair makes seeing difficult for the muskox but this is not the case. The muskox has excellent eyesight and can even see well in faint light. This is important because winter days on the tundra are very short and the nights are long. In the northernmost parts of the muskox's range, there may be no real daylight for weeks as the sun does not rise above the horizon.

As well, this shaggy wonder has a good sense of smell.

Too Heavy Means Too Hot

Imagine wearing a fur coat all summer long! Whew! You would get very, very hot, right? That is what happens to muskoxen in summer. Although they like to run and play, they soon become overheated because of their two protective coats.

When you get hot you perspire through millions of sweat glands that cover your body. But in its whole body, a muskox has only two sweat glands, located on its back feet. So the muskox cannot cool off by perspiring, and it gets hot and tired very quickly. It can only be active for a little while and then it must rest. If there are still mounds of snow around, a hot muskox may try to cool down by lying in one.

A young muskox's coat is short and curly.

Home on the Tundra

Muskoxen do not have special feeding areas as many other animals do. They do not even have a home where they sleep each night. Instead, they roam over the arctic plains, stopping wherever they find food.

In the summertime they look for places where the plants are lush and green. River valleys that have been covered with rich soil after a spring flood make good summer range for muskoxen because lots of plants grow there.

In the wintertime, muskoxen move to higher ground. They look for ridges or hills where the wind has blown away the snow, exposing grass or low bushes. But there is little food available in the winter, and the muskoxen may have to roam very far to get enough to eat.

In summer, muskoxen roam coastal plains and river valleys where food is most abundant.

Summer Salads

What do muskoxen eat? In the summer they dine on grasses and plants such as willowherb, knotweed, fleabane and bladder campion. The fresh green leaves of tiny arctic trees make a tasty treat. Although the tundra is almost always defined as "treeless," several kinds of trees, such as willow, birch and alder, do grow there. But they grow very slowly and never very big. A tree that's a hundred years old may be no more than a metre (3 feet) tall— which puts its leaves at a perfect height for a muskox to munch on.

Believe it or not, the muskox has no upper front teeth. To eat it must grip the food between its tongue or lower teeth and the roof of its mouth.

Frozen Dinner

In winter there is a lot less food available for the muskoxen, and most of it is covered with snow. Their winter food is mainly crowberry, bilberry, Labrador tea and the small, stunted trees of the tundra.

Sometimes, when the snow forms a thick crust over everything, the muskox must dig for food. It uses its sharp hoofs to paw through the icy snow. If that does not work, the muskox will use its head. Yes, its head! It will break the ice layer on the snow by pounding its head through the crust. Then it uses its hoofs to push away the broken ice chunks and get to the food below.

These muskoxen will have to work hard to find food here.

Very Impressive Horns

The muskox has a huge head crowned by a large pair of horns. The horns turn upwards and outwards. The tips are worn and polished while the rest of the horns are ribbed and ridged.

You can easily tell the female muskox from the bull if you look at the horns. The cow's horns are smaller, and they are separated by a patch of fur on the forehead. The bull's horns are larger and are very broad at the base where they join the forehead. This wide band of horn and the thick bone underneath protect the muskox's skull.

The horns are pale colored on a young muskox and turn dark brown as the animal gets older. It takes about six years for a muskox's horns to grow to their full adult size.

The horns tell it all. This is a young bull muskox.

Handy Hoofs

Ice and snow can be difficult to walk on unless you have special footwear. The muskox does. Its hoofs have sharp rims and rough heel pads that give it good traction on slippery surfaces.

In winter, fur grows on the heel pads for even more traction. And the hoofs are wide enough to help spread the muskox's great weight out over the snow. This helps to keep it from sinking in.

A muskox also finds its hoofs handy for something other than getting around. The front ones are larger than the back ones, and they make good shovels when the muskox must dig through the snow for food.

Muskoxen climb rocky slopes with ease.

31

Hoof prints

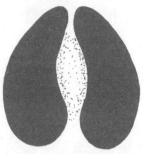

Front

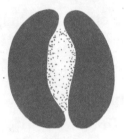

Hind

Good Company

Muskoxen generally travel in groups, or herds. A muskox herd may contain anywhere from 3 to 100 animals, but the average is 15.

The herds may change in size from time to time. A large herd may break into several smaller ones. Or a number of small herds may join together to form one large one. Usually the herds will be larger in winter. Sometimes, the herds will be made up mostly of females and their young, with the bulls wandering about alone or in small bachelor groups. Other times they will be mixed, male and female, young and old.

The more the merrier!

A Wall of Muskoxen

Muskoxen have very few enemies. The wolf is their main predator and the Grizzly Bear may also attack them. When threatened, they protect themselves by forming a tight circle with the calves at the center. The adults stand with their horned heads pointing out.

Instead of just waiting for the predator to leave, one or more bulls may rush from the circle to attack. They take turns doing this so that none ever gets too tired. The bulls are extremely agile and can run surprisingly fast as they try to gore or trample their attacker.

When it is very cold the muskoxen form a triangle. The bulls hunch up their shoulders and face into the wind. The calves and cows form the other two sides of the triangle, protected from the wind by the bulls.

Overleaf:
Defense formation.

Within the muskoxen's range, temperature of -45° Celsius (-50° Fahrenheit) are common in winter.

A Walking Icicle

After a heavy snowfall or sleet storm a
muskox often looks like a walking icicle.
Melting ice or snow sometimes forms icicles
which hang from the muskox's coat. The
muskox cannot bite off the icicles. Instead it
carries them around and they tinkle like bells
as the muskox walks.

Huddled together against the cold.

Mating Time

The cows and bulls mate in September, but
before this two males sometimes challenge
each other for the right to mate with a cow.
At this time, the male gives off the musky
odor that gave the animal its name. The scent
comes from a gland near the bull's eyes and he
spreads it over his front legs by rubbing them
with his head.

In late summer the tundra resounds with the
noise of battling males. The challengers charge
at each other and meet head-on with a
deafening crash. Fortunately most of the force
of the crash is absorbed by the muskox's thick
horns and skull.

The bulls continue to charge at each other
until one finally loses courage and veers off at
the last minute. If neither backs off, the bulls
continue to fight with head-to-head pushing,
hooking of horns and wrestling until one is so
exhausted he gives up.

Two heavy-weights square off.

Tundra Baby

The baby muskox is born in late April or early May, about eight months after the adults mate. This is still mid-winter in the Arctic, but the babies have to be born this early to allow them lots of time to grow up before next winter. Usually there is just one baby but some mothers have twins.

A newborn calf weighs about nine kilograms (20 pounds) which is about the weight of an adult raccoon. The baby begins to drink its mother's milk almost immediately. It gathers strength rapidly and is able to stand within minutes. In a few hours, it is strong enough to keep up with the herd.

"I'm the King of the Castle!"

Mother and Baby

The muskox is born with a short, curly dark brown coat. It does not grow long guard hairs like its parents until its third winter. Until then it must stick close to its mother and snuggle up to her warm side.

The mother only gives birth every other year and so she has lots of time to look after her baby. And what a fast growing baby! It begins nibbling tender grass shoots within a week of being born but continues to nurse on its mother's rich milk for over a year. By the time the calf is one year old it weighs 90 kilograms (200 pounds)—10 times what it weighed when it was born.

Although the young muskox is born with no horns at all, small bumps sprout on its forehead when it is about six months old. By the time it is a year old, the horns are six centimetres (2.5 inches) long, and at age two they are almost three times that long.

Fun and games.

Growing Up

The young calves like playing and racing about. They love to butt one another, and their favorite game is King of the Castle. One clambers to the top of a mound and paws the ground, challenging anyone to knock it off. Since it is just a game, no one gets hurt. Soon there is a new King of the Castle, and a new round of butting starts.

Butting games prepare the calves for battles when they are older, either with other muskoxen or against their enemies. The calves must grow up quickly in their arctic home. With the help of the rest of the herd they can live to be 20 years old and have several babies of their own.

Special Words

Bull   Male muskox.

Calf   Young muskox.

Cow   Female muskox.

Cud   Hastily swallowed food brought back for chewing by cud chewers such as cows, deer and muskoxen.

Fleece   The woolly inner layer of a muskox's coat.

Guard hairs   Long coarse hairs that make up the outer layer of the muskox's coat.

Hoofs   Feet of deer, goats, muskoxen and some other animals.

Mate   To come together to produce young.

Nurse   To drink milk from a mother's body.

Predator   Animal that hunts other animals for food.

Tundra   Vast northern plains.

INDEX

Cover Photo: Stephen J. Krasemann (Valan Photos)

Photo Credits: R. Harrington (Miller Services), page 4; Stephen J. Krasemann (Valan Photos), pages 7, 15, 16, 19, 20, 23, 29, 33, 40; Norman Lightfoot (Eco-Art Productions), pages 8, 12, 24; J.D. Taylor (Miller Services), page 11; Mike Beedele (Miller Services), page 26; Fred Bruemmer, pages 30, 34, 36-37, 38, 42, 45.